IMAGES OF ENGLAND

WALTON-ON-THAMES

IMAGES OF ENGLAND

WALTON-ON-THAMES

WENDY HUGHES

TEMPUS

To the people of Walton, past, present and future.

Frontispiece: Two residents take a reflective look at Walton's oldest building, the Parish Church of St Mary's. Based on magnetic compass variations, it has been suggested that the east/west alignment of the site may date from AD 700. The Domesday Survey of 1086 states that there was a church at Walton, although this was probably a small wooden building. The tower dates from around AD 1450, replacing an earlier one, but has been so frequently restored that it is difficult to date. Near a window is a rebus (enigmatic representation of a name) dated 1624, which no one has been able to decipher. The old clock was taken down in the 1890s and replaced with the present one, presented by Mr Richard Wilcox Boyle.

First published 2003

Tempus Publishing Limited
The Mill, Brimscombe Port,
Stroud, Gloucestershire, GL5 2QG

© Wendy Hughes, 2003

British Library Cataloguing in Publication Data.
A catalogue record for this book is available from the British Library.

ISBN 0 7524 3051 3

Typesetting and origination by Tempus Publishing Limited
Printed in Great Britain by Midway Colour Print, Wiltshire

Contents

Acknowledgements

I would like to thank the following people, in alphabetical order, for providing photographs and interesting information about Walton. Without their immense input I would not have been able to compile this book: Darren Bayley, Pat Bristow, Sid Brittin, June Byrne, Valerie Elam, Gerry Gilbert, Phillip and Alan Gosney, Geraldine Harvey, John Harvey, Ann and Bill Heffernan, Mrs Hickey, Marion Hitch, Keith Holdaway, Lesley Lambie, Brian and Guy Pollington, Jim Rosewell, Irene Sandells, Ronald and Susan Segal, John Stevens, Joan Wallace, Frank Wheals and Gwen Woodroff, as well as the Walton Society, and the Surrey Herald.

Special thanks must go to: Jeremy Hall who provided me with some excellent photographs and those taken at St Mary's and St John's churches are reproduced here with the permission of the vicar and churchwardens. Also thanks to Fred Lake who provided the postcards and information on Walton's film industry, Surrey Library Services for permission to reproduce photographs from their collection, Elmbridge Museum, Weybridge, part of Elmbridge Borough Council's Leisure and Cultural Services for permission to reproduce photographs from their collection and Jane Lewry of Elmbridge Borough Council for permission to use the Borough crest. Also, Ken Treanor Hon. Curator of the Royal NZ Army Medical Corps Museum, Christchurch, New Zealand for photographs of Mount Felix. Finally, thanks to Conrad Hughes who not only lived and breathed this book for so many months, but meticulously proofread the manuscript and helped me to avoid silly errors. Any that remain are my responsibility.

Introduction

Recently Walton-on-Thames has seen the publication of several excellent books on its ancient and colourful history. The area has changed considerably over the years, and even as this book is being compiled, changes are afoot in the town centre and at the parade of shops on Terrace Road. This book is not an attempt to produce more of the same, or an attempt at a history of the town, but aims to offer a collection of images to complement those books already in print, and possibly show a different aspect of the town that grew from a small Saxon settlement. Some of the photographs are modern by archive standards, but have been chosen because they show something that is no longer there, or depict the ever-changing face of the town.

Today Walton-on-Thames in the north-west of Surrey has a large commuter population, but evidence of its village origins that grew from a settlement are all around us. In fact a stroll around the Bridge Street and Manor Road area of the town will reveal much of Walton's past.

In ancient times the parish of Walton-on-Thames was part of the Hundred of Elmbridge, a Hundred being an administrative area of a shire. In 1974 it was decided that the Urban District of Walton-on-Thames and Weybridge, with a population of around 52,000 should be merged with the Urban District of Esher. The boundary of the new Borough coincided with that of the old ancient Hundred, so it was decided to call it the Borough of Elmbridge.

The name Walton is Anglo-Saxon in origin and is believed to mean 'farm of the Briton' or 'Saxon settlement', but even earlier it is believed to be the site of a Celtic settlement. The word Wealas refers to the Celtic inhabitants who lived here before the Anglo-Saxons. Waletona as it was spelt then is mentioned in the Domesday Survey of 1086 as having a church, two mills and a fishery.

By way of an introduction to this historic town, I offer a few highlights through history. Prehistoric finds have been made in the neighbourhood of Walton, especially along the riverside, proving that the town was once a Saxon settlement because an iron spearhead with socket and shaft was found opposite Tumbling Bay, by G.R. Hayward in 1952, in about one inch of earth on the recreational ground at the end of Dudley Road.

There must have been great excitement in Elizabethan Walton when in 1568 William Camden located the stakes at Cowey Stake, and publicised his theory that this was where Julius Caesar crossed the Thames on his second invasion of Britain. In the eighteenth century, William Stukeley published a plan showing Caesar's camp at Walton-on-Thames, 1 August in 54 BC.

St Mary's Church, the oldest building in Walton, has stood for over 1,000 years on the low hill overlooking the river, and has many historical monuments, each telling its own unique story. The Old Manor House is a fine example of a fourteenth-century half-timbered building lovingly restored and used as a family home. The Tudor builders did much for Walton, and in 1516 Henry VIII granted a licence to hold a fair at Walton. The River Thames has always played a major role in the town's history, with some residents such as the Rosewells, making their living from it. Until 1750 the river could only be crossed by ford or ferry until Samuel Dicker built a wooden toll bridge, and payable tolls only ended in 1870. One of the tollhouses can be seen today on the Shepperton side of the bridge. Thames Cottage, with its deeds dated 1747, once the ferryman's cottage with stabling behind, is now Long Cottage.

The nineteenth and twentieth centuries brought about changes to the area, turning Walton from a predominately rural farming community to a small town, especially when the railway arrived, and the houses opened up their fronts as shops. Before the First World War, roads were unmade and were watered down in the summer to stem the dust. This was also the age of the birth of the silent film industry, and Cecil Hepworth and Walton played a major role in its development. The Power Brothers also contributed hugely to the development of dental equipment worldwide, and became one of the biggest employers in the town.

In 1900 Walton's population was 10,300, and in 1904 a cottage hospital, supported by voluntary contributions, opened in Sidney Road. At about this time electric light also came to Walton, supplied by the Urban Electric Supply Company, and by 1906 some of the streets in Walton were lit by electricity. By 1911 the number of registered users was approximately 600.

Between the wars Ashley House Estate was sold and resulted in the widening of the High Street and the building of luxury homes on the estate. Walton's character underwent another change after the Second World War, and again in the 1960s with the opening up of Hepworth Way and the building of the centre. Concerns about the number of notable buildings being lost forever resulted in the formation of Walton Society in 1975. The society has done much to preserve the character of Walton and respect for it is shown through its representation on the Borough Council where it is the largest group.

At the time of writing, Walton is under the cloud of further change as we patiently wait for news on the second phase of the new shopping centre. It is hoped that future generations will look upon books, like this one, and view a glimpse of Walton that has been lost forever.

Wendy Hughes – Walton-on-Thames
June 2003

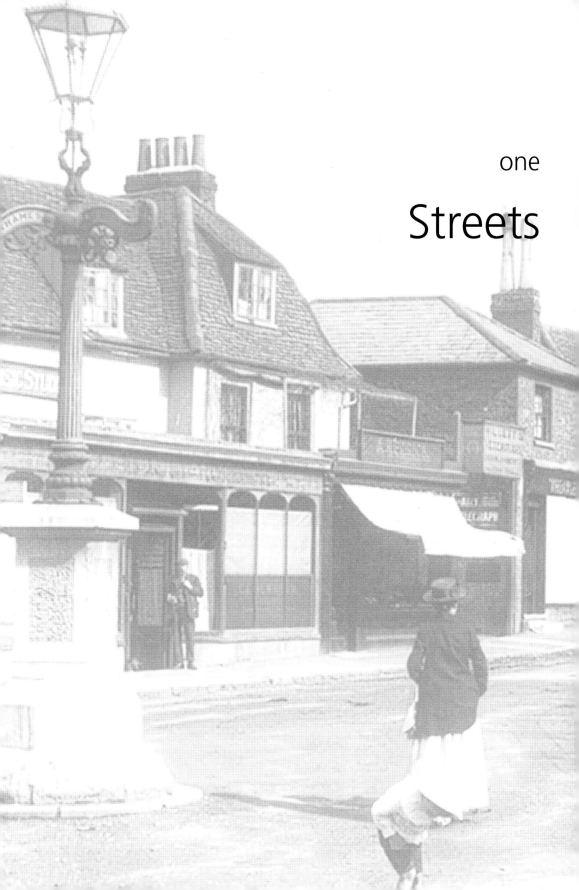

one

Streets

Church Street, the widest of the three shopping streets, stretches from St Mary's Church to the junction with High Street. When this photograph was taken in 1897 this was the main shopping street and remained so until the High Street was developed in the 1920s. Left of the picture is the wood-faced building of Bennett and Co., coachbuilder, and further up the street is Charles Hurst's grocery business. Opposite the post office can be seen next to the Dolphin. Outside John Seaby's horse-drawn fly business – forerunner of today's taxis – can be seen a horse trough, no doubt frequented by Seaby's horses. Further up the road, under the awning is the saddle harness business of William E. Birkhead.

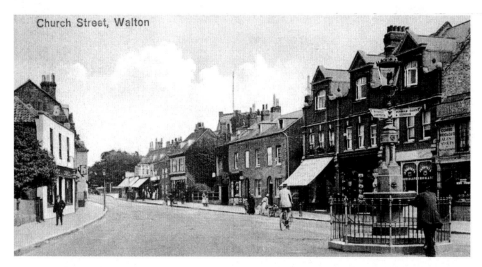

Church Street, Walton

This postcard shows the drinking fountain, erected in 1899, a gift to the people of Walton from Richard Wilcox Boyle. Because of vandalism by local children, railings were erected in 1906. This postcard taken around 1910 shows a new row of shops, built around 1902 to replace the white-fronted shops seen in the previous photograph. Initially Merrick's Dairy, Adam Bell's gentlemen's outfitters, and a jeweller occupied these. Mr Bell took over his shop on 15 May 1907 and ran it until 1932, when it passed to his son Roland and daughter-in-law Phyllis, who passed the business on to their two daughters in 1960. The shop closed in 1974 and was demolished to make way for Barclays bank.

This view looking down Church Street around 1890 shows, near the boy on the right, Henry Wheatley's barber salon where customers' shaving mugs and brushes were kept in rows on a shelf around the shop. Henry Dale and Co., the biggest butcher in the village, is facing up Church Street, with several carcasses hanging outside. The animals were slaughtered at the bottom of the yard behind the shop, usually during the afternoon after the deliveries. In 1906 the business became J. Ive, and remained a butcher's under E. Grimditch from 1922 until the building was demolished in 1963.

Here we see Bridge Street, Walton's second shopping street, in 1903. In the centre of the picture we see the George Public House, with Brooking's small grocery shop next door, where it was possible to buy a penny rasher, a penny worth of vinegar or just one egg. On the right is Phillipson's bookbinding and lending library, soon to become Edmund Jordan's. On the left is A.D. Coopers drapery business, a large double-fronted shop, which was taken over by Mr Palmer, who sold china and glass in one half, whilst his son, who was later killed in the First World War, ran an outfitters in the other.

Above: Looking along Bridge Street around 1910, can be seen the offices of C.E. Newham, solicitor's and commissioner of oaths, on the left, with a music studio above. Next door under the awning is Alfred Merrick's greengrocer's shop. Behind is Willett's Veterinary establishment and shoeing forge, then Ralph Wheatley, coach builder. The Star Brewery, which was acquired by Brandon's Putney Brewery Ltd in 1897 is used as a depot. Brewing had ceased on the premises by the time this photograph was taken. The street lamp was erected in 1898 having been removed from Church Street to make way for the fountain.

Opposite, above: This historic photograph showing the pulling down of George Turner's cycle business, started in 1899, to make Hepworth Way an extension of Church Street. According to many older residents, this spelt the end of the Walton they knew and loved.

Opposite, below: This sketch of High Street around 1870 looking down towards Bridge Street shows the trees and tall wall surrounding the Ashley Park Estate. Horse fairs were once held in the High Street.

13

By 1908 the High Street is beginning to look more like a shopping street as more houses became shops, but we can still see the Ashley Park estate on the left-hand side. Miss Gladys Ward, who came to Walton in 1898 aged ten and left her memoirs to Walton, could remember a little sweet shop set into the wall of Ashley Park. Directly opposite the gates is Powers, the chemist at number 9, whose three sons, Edward, George and Henry, combined their profession as dentists with the manufacture of dental equipment in the shed behind the shop. In 1888 they patented an adjustable stool or seat for use by dentists. The ornate shop on the corner is Timothy White's and opposite, on the same side of the road, can be seen Walton Village Hall. In 1879 Mrs Sassoon of Ashley Park donated £1,200 for the erection of a public hall, a gift to the people of Walton to commemorate the marriage of her son Joseph, in 1880.

A farm has stood on this site in the High Street adjoining the United Dairies, opposite the war memorial since at least 1820. This photograph taken around 1890 shows William Reed's son 'Gaffer,' a keen sportsman who enjoyed rowing, running, boxing, weight-lifting and climbing the greasy pole! As children, Gaffer and his brother C.J. had been climbing boys in their father's chimney sweep business and had even climbed the chimney at Ashley Park House.

This postcard of High Street in the mid-1950s shows the Builders Arms, that was renamed the Kiwi to commemorate the links forged with New Zealand in the First World War. It closed for refurbishment and re-opened on 4 November 1956 as the Kiwi, advertising luncheons and evening meals. On the left-hand side, where Ashley Road and New Zealand Avenue now join, used to be a pound, a small square paddock, surrounded by a timber cross-bar fence tarred black. Any animals found straying in the streets were taken to the pound, and the owners had to pay a fee to have them released.

This photograph shows the Capitol Cinema, decorated for the Coronation of George VI in 1937. The Capitol Cinema opened in 1927 with Clifford Spain, who worked for Hepworth as actor, cameraman and projectionist, as manager. Spain also made and screened his own newsreels of local interest until he left to manage Walton's Regal Cinema.

This photograph, taken in the 1970s, looks towards the distinctive shape of Ireton's house, which previously was Mac Fisheries but is now a motor factor's shop. The High Street is busy with shoppers, which suggests that it could be a Friday or Saturday morning.

A rather quiet King's Road taken in 1909, where the only traffic to worry about was the occasional horse and cart. The road was probably named in honour of the new King Edward VII in 1901.

New Zealand Avenue around 1959. On the right can been seen the Regal cinema advertising *Jet Storm*, released August 1959, starring Richard Attenborough and Diane Cilento. This 2,000-seat super-cinema had an exact replica of the BBC theatre organ, and Reginald Fort came to Walton to play at the opening ceremony.

In the early 1970s two projects lead to local protests, and the founding of the Walton Society. Birkheads site, seen here closed and boarded up, had stood in Church Street for as long as residents could remember. After an unsuccessful campaign it, together with Snell's drapers shop, was gone forever, replaced by Safeway's supermarket. The second project involved the building of flats alongside the Thames, which many claimed would ruin the view of the Thames and restrict access. Following a public meeting in November 1975, which attracted 250 people, the Walton Society emerged with, amongst others, an objective dedicated to maintaining the character of the town.

Church Walk, pictured here in the 1980s, was once known as Church Alley and led from St Mary's to the High Street, opposite an entrance to Ashley House. This ancient right of way, used by the occupants of Ashley House, still exists although new houses have been built.

two

Shops

A harness-making business was established on this site in 1750 by William and Charles Giles. In 1890 William Edgar Birkhead bought the business and ran it with a staff of four. By 1915 he was making cycles and by the 1930s he also sold sports goods. In 1939 the business became a limited company, shortly before this photograph was taken. In the 1950s a record department was added advertising Birkhead's as 'His Master's Voice' record dealer. By 1972 Birkhead's was a department store with a staff of forty selling electrical goods, sports equipment, leather goods, baby clothes and kitchen units to name but a few. By the 1980s it was demolished.

William Gray's boot repairing business in Church Street closed in 1914, shortly after this picture was taken. The building was pulled down to make way for Walton's first purpose-built cinema, which opened in 1915.

This Dutch gabled building at the top end of the High Street, photographed around 1910, dates probably from the seventeenth century and is known locally as Ireton's house. It is said that General Henry Ireton, a roundhead military commander who married Bridget, one of Cromwell's daughters in 1646, lived here, but this is not proven.

Thomas Purdue moved from Shepperton in around 1900 to manage Readings, a fishmonger and poulterer shop at number 47 High Street. In this picture we see him with his daughter Winnie and son Henry, seated on the newly acquired delivery tricycle, outside their house at 48 Annett Road around 1910.

This photograph shows numbers 13, 15 and 17 Church Street, with the former Palace Cinema, now Cyril Gall's furniture shop set back. Residents and employees in shops and offices in Church Street formed a fire-watching rota during the Second World War, and met in the rooms over the WVS offices in the former House and Ager building, which was opposite the Church.

This photograph of Huntley Brothers was taken around 1920. Mr Lycett, the manager, is in the doorway. Huntley Brothers was known to most children as the place to buy school uniforms, and remained in business until the 1980s.

Adam Charles Bell stands proudly outside his shop, soon after taking over from Colliers in 1907. At the time the stock and debts were valued at £455 12s 2d and the lease and goodwill at £175. In February 1955 Mr Corbin Ward was manager of A.C. Bell's, and the business continued until the shop was demolished to make way for Barclays bank in 1974.

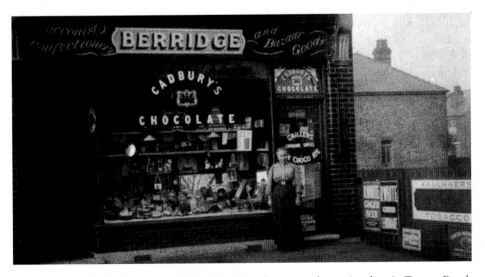

According to Kelley's directory of 1913, Alfred Berridge ran a tobacconists shop in Terrace Road at the corner of Russell Road, where the laundrette is now. This photograph, taken in the 1920s, could include Mrs Berridge. By now they also sold confectionery and bazaar goods.

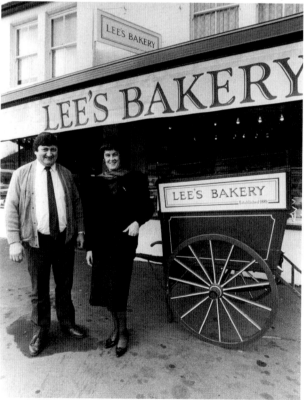

Above: Daniel Pollington started his well-known newsagents in 1934. The business passed to his son, Leslie, pictured in the 1930s. He in turn handed the business with shops at The Halfway and Oatlands to his three sons, Keith, Brian and Tony. Over the years, Pollingtons has provided pocket money to hundreds of Walton youngsters, who were employed as paperboys and papergirls.

Left: Lee's Bakery has stood on these premises at the corner of Terrace Road and Sunbury Lane since Samuel Lee opened the business in 1899. This photograph, taken in the 1980s, shows the present owners, Bill and Anne Heffernan, who took over the business in 1973 and were voted Britain's All Round Champion Bakery 1996/97.

Around 1870 the houses at the Halfway were being converted into shops, and in 1875 Louis Phillipe Millican, who worked as a baker's boy at Bethnal Green in London, married the baker's daughter, Esther Mary Ann Cox. At the time Louis' brother was a gardener at Ashley Park, and told Louis that he thought Walton was a good place to start up a business. He began by putting his first baker's dozen, thirteen loaves, in the front room window of his house in Hersham Road. This photograph shows a new shop front, c. 1900. At this time an oven was installed at the back, which is still in place today. Over the years the shop has served several bakeries, including a branch of Lees.

Snells, the three-storied drapers shop, on the right-hand side of Church Street around 1937, can be remembered by many older residents for its beautiful wood floors and the place to buy up-to-date hats. Here the assistant would place money and the sales docket in a tube, then tug a lever sending the account transaction whizzing along a wire to the office whilst the customer waited for its return to receive their change. When it was pulled down in the 1970s an attempt to preserve the Edwardian frontage failed when it collapsed.

Above: Joseph Blake, draper and silk mercer, opened a shop on this site in Church Street in 1843. This photograph shows the shop, rebuilt in 1903, with a flag flying from its roof, *c.* 1925. On 14 March 1944 incendiary bombs that also damaged the church destroyed it. The roof of the Castle Inn next door was so badly damaged that it had to be replaced with a flat roof but the inn continued to trade until 1972 before being demolished the next year.

Left: The Fountain Bookshop, seen here around 1960, owned by Mr M.W. Dashwood, was opened on 10 July 1954, in New Zealand Avenue. He specialised in children's books and built his display from the ground up – toddlers' titles on the bottom with the higher shelves reserved for the older and taller children. To interest the adults, Sir Harold Scott, author of the new *Scotland Yard* bestseller opened the proceedings with Annette Mills, creator of Muffin, signing books for children. Also present was Miss Rose Fyleman, the poet and author who told the world, 'There are fairies at the bottom of my garden.' In 1956 the shop was extended to twice its original size to form a special children's room. It closed in the 1980s.

Number 85 High Street, known as Osborne House, was a high-class provision merchant and family grocer for many years. This photograph taken around 1925 shows one of the company's vans waiting to take out a delivery. It was one of the largest shops in Walton, serving most of the large houses. Fred Wood, who opened his shop in 1913, remained there until 1930. It subsequently became the Co-op until it was demolished for redevelopment.

Pics and Things, run by Mr and Mrs Hinchcliffe, was a delightful shop selling anything to do with pictures and framing, and stood in Church Walk just off the High Street. This photograph was taken in the 1980s just before the shop was demolished to make way for new housing.

George Turner came to Walton around 1870, began his cycle business in 1889 and produced the Walton Cycle here in 1900. During the First World War, soldiers recuperating at the New Zealand Hospital, would hire cycles to explore the local countryside. Turner branched out into motorcycle and car repairs, which became his principal trade. In 1905 he also moved into the radio business, selling phonographs and cylinder records. The business remained a family concern until 1963. This photograph taken around 1960 also shows Burtons, above which was a dance hall called the High Spot, and a restaurant.

Kenneth G. Haynes owned the Pet Shop in New Zealand Avenue seen here around the 1970s. It was always an attraction for children with a variety of animals on display in the windows, as well as a huge selection of goldfish and over 2,000 tropical fish inside. It is now Walton Cycles.

Right: Over the years, several estate agents have occupied Admiral Rodney House, as can be seen here in this 1957 photograph. Named after George Brydges Rodney who is believed to have been was born here in 1719, he later went on to become a naval hero in 1782 when he won a victory over the French fleet of Admiral de Grasse off Dominica. In 1932 St Mary's Church celebrated the 150th anniversary of that victory by flying the white ensign from the tower, but officials instructed that it be taken down as the church was neither a ship nor a naval vessel.

Below: The Studio Gallery in Bridge Street, seen here in 1970s is where the cartoonist Bill Wright had his studios.

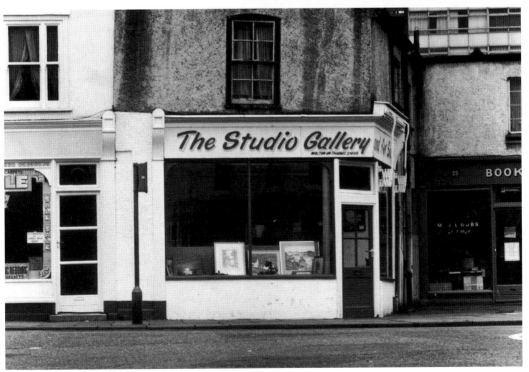

Above: This 1957 photograph shows the Singer Sewing Machine shop, which had operated here for over fifty years before moving to the corner of High Street. Note the beautiful seventeenth- or early eighteenth-century Venetian windows and also the ornate lamp standard on the bus stop, where passengers would have taken the bus to Molesey and Kingston.

Right: This close-up picture was taken when the ornate lamp standard – possibly the last in Walton – was taken down at Church Walk to make way for the new housing, *c.* 1970.

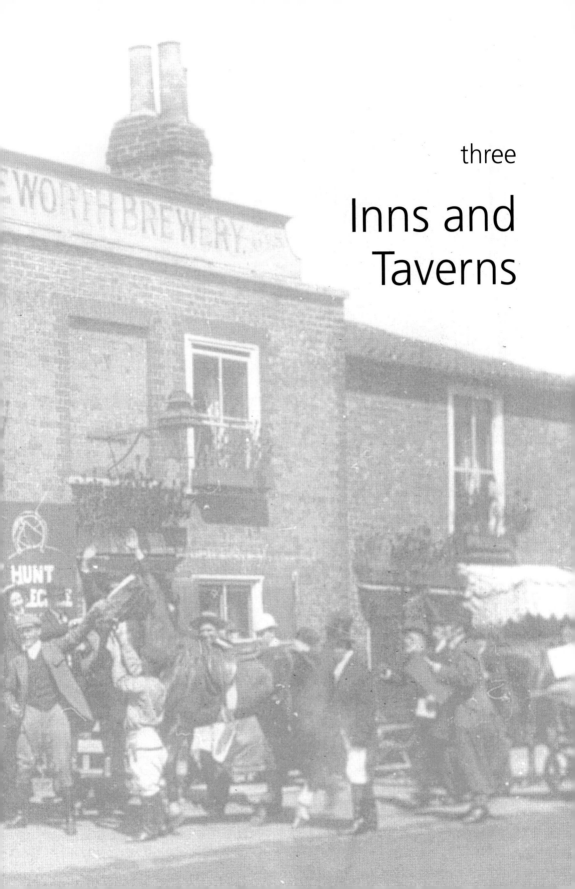

three

Inns and Taverns

The building shown here bears the name Ye Olde Bear Inn. At various times it has been known as the Bear, the White Bear, Brown Bear and the Old Bear. The earliest reference to the Bear is 1729 when Elizabeth Sanders was licensed to keep an alehouse. This Inn is significant for early Congregationalists in Walton who hired the clubroom and on 29 September 1839 the Revd A.E. Lord preached the first sermon. Services continued for five years despite local opposition. During the early 1900s the actors and technicians from Walton film studios came here for lunch.

The Anglers was first mentioned as a public house in a deed of 1870. Prior to this date Anglers Cottage stood on this site. In 1869 the widow of J.W. Foulkes sold the cottage to John Trotter, who leased it to Mr J.J. Herbert in 1870 for use as a public house. John Trotter sold the freehold to Brandon Putney Brewery Ltd, who owned it at the time this photograph was taken in 1900.

The Old Manor Inn can be seen here with the Old Manor House in the background. This eighteenth-century building probably was previously a dwelling house. The original application for a licence was granted in March 1866 to John Rosewell and supported by the local clergy and churchwardens. He appears to have been the innkeeper until at least 1878.

Apps Court Tavern stood on the junction of Walton Road and Hurst Road and was reconstructed after a fire in 1865. At this time the occupier was Ephraim Bridges and the owner was W.F. Hodgson. In 1870 the then landlord Edward Bridges had his licence withdrawn for selling brandy outside permitted hours in accordance with the annual licensing sessions. This photograph shows Bertha Kemp on the steps, *c.* 1939. The landlord Thomas Kemp was there from 1924 to June 1944. It was closed after the war and finally demolished in 1965.

Top left: According to Ryde's map of 1865, the owner of the George Public House in Bridge Street was Sarah Coothorn and the occupier was George James. It was apparently rebuilt in 1888, hence the inscription in the red brick work. There was an alehouse in Walton known as the George in 1729 when John Taylor was a licensee, although no connection with this George has been proven.

Below left: During the late nineteenth century there were about twelve inns and taverns in Walton, and another way of dealing with those who had one too many was to make the offender parade through the streets wearing a barrel as illustrated here.

Opposite, below: In 1890 Joseph Sassoon who had opened a Golf Club in Ashley Park sold land to Friary Holroyd and Healy's Brewery on which to build a hotel. In March 1891 the licensing authority granted a licence on the understanding that the New Inn in nearby Oatlands Park would be closed. The landlord, Mr James Hedges, became the landlord of the Ashley Park Hotel. When the hotel opened Sassoon agreed to open up a footpath from the town centre to the station through his land. However, in 1898 the newly-formed Walton Council ordered him to remove barbed wire placed across the path. This postcard, postmarked Walton-on-Thames 15 January 1917, has two crosses marked either side of a window. On the back of the card is written 'Vera's sitting room.' The card is also advertising the L and SW Railway – Walton to Waterloo in thirty minutes.

The Drunkard's Cloak

An old form of Punishment for persons convicted of Tippling. Prisoners were paraded through the Streets in a tub.

COPYRIGHT

The Swan Hotel, Walton on Thames.   4094-247

An Inn has stood on this site since 1769. The present Swan, a brick and half-timbered building with a tiled roof and a spire, appears to have been built around the 1870s, replacing a small eighteenth-century building. At one time the Swan had its own landing stage on the riverbank, and at the time this photograph was taken which was around 1908, the landlord's daughter, Eva Leale fell in love with a customer who arrived by boat. He was the American composer Jerome Kern, and they were married at St Mary's Church on 25 October 1910. Eva was only eighteen at the time and the couple lived briefly at 76 Manor Road before leaving for America. Whilst filming at Walton studios Stewart Rome lodged at the Swan.

Ashley Park Hotel, Walton-on-Thames.
Tel. 196. 30 Minutes Waterloo L. & S. W. Rly.

The Plough Inn traded from 1778 in two eighteenth-century cottages. This picture dates from 1909 and was taken during the filming of 'The Race For The Farmer's Cup', a 725ft silent film lasting eleven and a half minutes. The hero, the farmer, won the race and the girl, and was played by Lewin Fitzamon (1869-1961), a former steeplechase jockey who used to act when a horseman was needed. The building was demolished in 1928.

This is the building that replaced the one in the previous photograph. Here we see the pub when its name was changed in 1985 to the Last Viceroy, a rare photograph because within weeks it reverted to the Plough.

The earliest reference to the Duke's Head Hotel is in land and tax records dated 1792. At one time it featured a skittle ally at the end of the garden. It closed in 1966 when the present Duke's Head opened in Hepworth Way. During demolition work in 1970 a brick dated 1791 was discovered. Woolworth's now stands on this site.

The Builders Arms can be traced back to the annual licensing sessions for 1871 when a spirit licence was refused. However, by 1876 Phillipson's Directory lists R.G. Hoply as the innkeeper. This picture was taken in the 1920s before the building was replaced by the present red-bricked building. In 1956 the name was changed to the Kiwi and in 1986 changed again to the Wellington, after the town in New Zealand.

Until 1875 the Weir Hotel was known as the New Inn. This photograph was taken around 1906 soon after it was rebuilt following a fire that destroyed the building. Until 1994 it took in paying guests when it then became known simply as The Weir. This pub is particularly popular in summer months when boats can moor nearby, and a meal and drink can be enjoyed in the garden.

The Crown Hotel occupied the corner of Church Street and High Street since at least 1729, and can be seen here around 1914. The original building was of sixteenth-century construction with a late seventeenth- or early eighteenth-century façade. It was demolished in 1961. The Crown like many of the pubs in Walton ran a club through which members could obtain sick benefit when ill; the remaining funds being shared out at Christmas. This was long before the NHS and statutory sick pay.

four

Houses Great
and Small

The caption on this nineteenth-century print refers to the legend that claims that the Old Manor House once belonged to John Bradshaw, President of the Court who signed the death warrant of Charles I. No evidence has been found to confirm or dispute this view and so the legend goes on.

This 1970s photograph shows the interior of the Old Manor House. Advice sought by the present owner, Mr Ronald Segal, has confirmed that the original structure dates from around 1327 and the house has been listed a Grade 1 building, rare for a family home. The beams and the Minstrel's gallery, seen here, are original whereas the staircase most definitely is not.

Above and below: These recent photographs of the Old Manor House show the back (above) and front (below) of the house. As a result of its orientation the back is often mistakenly photographed as the front. Note the original wood and the uneven roof.

In the 1990s Mr Segal discovered a bulge in one of the bedroom ceilings, and called in an expert to deal with the problem. This was found to be a false ceiling that covered the 1327 original with its beams and coloured plasterwork.

Charles Bennet, Fourth Earl of Tankerville acquired the Mount Felix estate in 1772, and was the driving force behind Surrey County Cricket Club. He died in 1822, and the estate passed to his widow. The Tankerville crest, here photographed in 1970, can still be seen, although the estate has long gone.

In 1836, Charles, the Fifth Earl of Tankerville, inherited the estate and the following year engaged Charles Barry to redesign the house in the Italianate style. This postcard, produced in 1914 by Jon Edwards of Walton-on-Thames, shows the long double-storey building with a tiled roof and a square 70ft tower with a porch beneath.

This wintry photograph, taken around 1916, shows Mount Felix during the First World War when it was used as a New Zealand Military Hospital. This would have been the first time that many of these soldiers recovering from wounds received at Gallipoli would have seen snow.

A fire severely damaged Mount Felix in 1966, and most of it had to be demolished. The only part to survive, originally a brew house and laundry and then the carriage house, is known as the Clock Tower. The clock has been restored to working order and is seen here in the late 1970s.

Lady Jane Berkeley built Ashley House, a Jacobean dwelling seen here in the 1920s, between 1602 and 1607. Its last owners were the Sephardic Jewish Sassoon family. David Sassoon had built up a trading empire in India and the Far East and bought the house in 1860. When his eldest son Joseph died in 1922 the estate had no heir and so was broken up and sold. Subsequently, in 1935, New Zealand Avenue was constructed on the land.

Above: This photograph shows the entrance hall and gallery of Ashley House that had remained relatively unaltered for 300 years, *c.* 1923. The windows would appear to be eighteenth century.

Below: Ashley House was demolished in 1929, and these advertisements from 1930 show how the estate had been divided up into plots offered for sale at £400 per half acre.

ASHLEY PARK ESTATE
WALTON - ON - THAMES, *Surrey.*

Local Rates are only 7/– in the £, and the assessments are reasonable.

Company's Gas, Water, Electric Power for cooking, heating and lighting, also Main Drainage are laid in Silverdale Avenue and Ashley Drive — together with electric street lamps and underground telephone cables.

There are ample facilities in the district for Educational purposes for Boys and Girls.

Magnificent woodland Plots with varieties of beautiful trees are for sale at £400 per half acre, and there are also many attractive labour saving new houses built and in course of construction, for sale at cheap prices based on present day building costs.

For PHOTOGRAPHS OF THE ESTATE and Houses, Plans, etc., apply to :

A. BRASSEY TAYLOR
Bridge House,
181 Queen Victoria Street, London
'Phone: Central 1335 ; Walton 1180.   E.C.4
or on the Estate.

ASHLEY PARK ESTATE
WALTON-ON-THAMES, Surrey

IN a health-giving locality favoured for its pines and recuperating qualities, this BEAUTIFUL RESIDENTIAL ESTATE, by the artistic and painstaking development of its Owners affords some of the most picturesque and magnificent Woodland Sites it is possible to find.

The Estate which is situate about 17 miles from London and within the West End of London daily delivery area, adjoins the charming old-world town on the North, and extends to the South within five minutes' walk of Walton Station, being bounded on all sides with very high-class and attractive Residential properties.

Above: In the 1890s, Elm Grove was leased to Prince Louis of Battenberg, a naval advisor at the War Office. His wife, Victoria of Hesse was Queen Victoria's favourite grand-daughter. In the summer of 1894, Prince Louis' brother Henry and wife Beatrice, and Queen Victoria's youngest sister, Alexandra (Alix) visited. In June the party were joined by Alix's fiancé Nicholas, who was to become the last fateful Tsar of Russia. In 1921 the Urban District Council bought the house to use as offices and an extension for a council chamber was built. The grounds were also laid out as a public park with a bowling green and tennis courts. When the Council was enlarged in 1932, Elm Grove continued to be used until the new town hall was built. This photograph, from 1957, relates to that period. Today the building is leased to Stagecoach drama school.

During restoration at Thames Cottage in 1968, little wooden animals were discovered between the beams. As they are of the same material it can be surmised that the men building the cottage in 1747 must have made them, perhaps in their lunch breaks.

Above: This photograph shows Long Cottage, which was originally the stables belonging to Thames Cottage and where the horses would have rested before taking the ferry across the Thames.

Opposite, below: The deeds for Thames Cottage date from 1747. At that time there would have been an entrance on the left-hand side of the main building for the coach and horses to go through to the stables at the back and on to the river for transportation by ferry. This left-hand side of the building has a regency bottom and a Victorian top indicating modernisation. When the present owner bought the cottage in 1968 a religious text was discovered in the plasterwork that suggests that at some time travellers praying for a safe journey could possibly have used it as a chapel. This photograph dates from 1970 after the restoration.

This gatehouse, pictured in 1970, at the end of Crutchfield Lane still stands and marks the entrance to Edward Peppin's carriage drive. The main house, Walton Lodge, which stood where Stuart Avenue meets Sidney Road, was an early eighteenth-century house said to have been designed by Vanburgh. Peppin briefly became the largest landowner in Walton and served as sheriff of Surrey from 1802.

Hillington House, seen here in 1903, was formally 56 Station Avenue and was designed by Nevin and Wigglesworth in 1899. The auction sale catalogue for 10 June 1925 describes the house as Queen Anne style, built of red brick with bold circular bay windows. By 1932 its name had changed to Tadcaster House and was up for sale for £5,000. In 1952 Mr E.S. Laurie who, in 1954, applied to Kingston upon Thames County Court for permission to build flats on the site acquired it. The house eventually was demolished in 1965.

Photographed around the turn of the century are residents of these old almshouses located at the corner of West Grove.

More modern cottages and a caretaker's lodge, seen here in the 1920s, later replaced the almshouses. They have now been demolished to make way for Mayfield Old People's Home.

This postcard issued by Sillence of Hersham Road around 1900 shows Ingram's Cottage over a century earlier. It stood on the corner of Ryden's Road and Hersham Road, opposite Halfway Green. The spot was later occupied by Cherry's Chemist shop and is now a dry-cleaning business.

The name Apps is first mentioned as part of lands given in 675 to the Abbey at Chertsey by St Erconward, then Bishop of London. Sometime before 1212, the tenant paid money into charity and each All Saint's day the owner handed out loaves and beer to the people. This photograph of Apps Court, taken in the 1880s shows the house that John Hamborough rebuilt in 1824. Robert Gill, a railway engineer, involved with George Stephenson in the construction of the Manchester and Leeds railway, and president of the Great Western Railway of Canada, then bought the property. He died in 1871 and in 1898 his widow, Fanny, sold the property and land to the Southward and Vauxhall Water Company and Apps Court disappeared into the Knights and Bessborough Reservoirs.

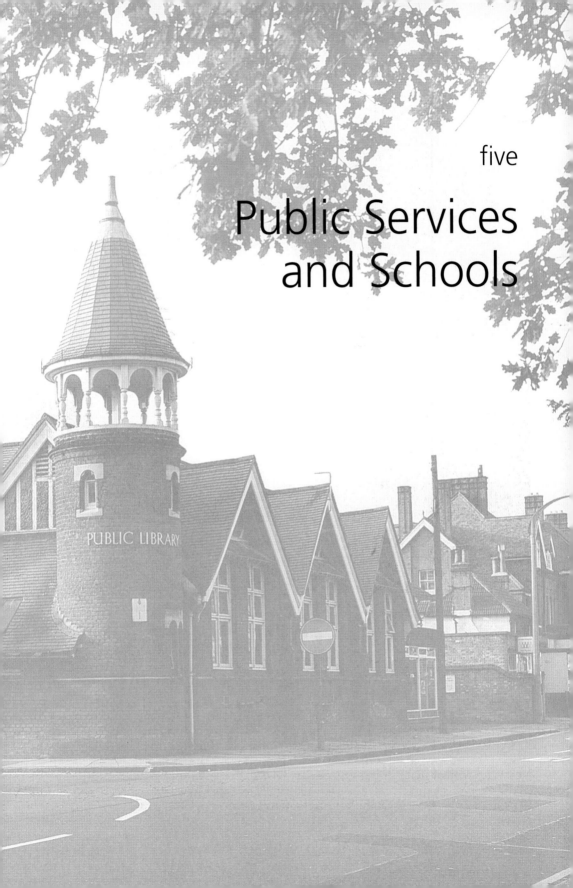

five

Public Services
and Schools

This line drawing from around 1900 shows Miskins Yard. In 1885 George Miskin took over a bench-saw and a traction engine from his father Thomas and established a wood business at the corner of Sidney Road and Terrace Road. In 1921 the business was amalgamated with James and Fredrick Gridley of Kingston and continued trading at the two sites as Gridley and Miskin Co. Ltd.

Mr Harry (Jo) Woodroff seen here in 1910, worked for Walton-on-Thames Urban District Council (formed in 1894). Most of the roads were unmade and became very dusty in summer. Mr Woodroff was employed to water the roads.

Because of local opposition, Walton Station was built away from the town centre. This rare photograph from around 1888 shows the station with just two tracks, but by 1895 it had been rebuilt with four tracks and a central platform.

As well as working for Miskins, Arthur Hirons also carried out contracting work for Walton Urban District Council as well as hiring out horses and carts. Arthure is seen here on the far right in Crutchfield Lane with his wife, who tended the horses ready for a 6 a.m. start, c. 1906.

This photograph taken around 1911 shows the last horse-drawn coach used by the Royal Mail between Walton, Hersham and Shepperton. The driver is George Fredrick Reed; elder brother of 'Gaffer Reed.' The horse was called Roger.

After a gale damaged the lamp and direction sign on top of the drinking fountain in Church Street, a lamp standard replaced it and the fountain moved to Elm Grove Recreation Ground in 1930 where it still stands.

Dr George White Drabble of Manor House in Church Street (where Court's Furniture is now) gave freehold land at the corner of Sidney Road and Rodney Road to build Walton, Hersham and Oatlands Cottage Hospital. The hospital was built in 1906 and underwent several extensions before being demolished in 1993.

Rodney House, opened in March 1928, was Walton's first Maternity Home, with Dr Drabble contributing £5,000 towards its £11,500 building costs. Actress Julie Andrews, who starred in *The Sound of Music*, was born here in 1935. The building, seen here at the end of its life, was demolished to make way for Walton Community Hospital.

Members of the volunteer Fire Brigade outside their station in High Street around 1909 which had previously been a lock-up given to them in 1876 by Walton Vestry and later rebuilt. Local tradesmen such as the Annett Bros (builders), Thomas Purdue (fishmonger) and William Birkhead (saddler) gave their services.

The first Earl of Ellesmere, owner of St George's Hill donated land to the parish of Walton for a free convalescent home for poor patients. The building, seen here in 1906, was opened in 1854 and provided accommodation for 300 patients. Two further wings were added in 1863 and 1868. The number of beds decreased over the years and after the NHS was set up it became a geriatric hospital before closing its doors to the developers in 1989.

Over a period of two years, Riverhouse Barn, a derelict barn once belonging to the Riverhouse Estate, has been restored to a state as near as possible to the original. This photograph taken in 1986 shows the barn at the start of restoration.

The barn was opened in 1989 and is the only centre fully devoted to the arts in the Borough of Elmbridge. It provides a venue for touring drama and music, and has exhibition space for professional artists and for local amateur arts clubs. This photograph taken in 1988 shows the extensive work carried out in two years.

The library seen here around 1960 has been at this site since 1932. From 1884 to 1931 this was Walton Infants' School which then moved to Ambleside Avenue.

This photograph taken at the Central school in 1930 shows Walter (Wally) Griffiths in front with Leslie Woodroff (third in the row) during a science lesson.

A class at Ashley Road School in 1922 shows Walter Griffiths, the second child along from the teacher, Mrs Matthews.

The Central School (a mixed school) became Mayfield Girls' School when the boys' school was opened in Ambleside Avenue in 1938. This photograph taken in 1955 shows Mr Bartlett's class. Pupils known are: Gloria McCarthy, Edna Winchester, Maureen Lampon, Margaretta Davies, Valerie Anscombe, June Harris, June Howard and Joan Boast.

This photograph shows Miss Reardon's class at Ashley Road School in 1950. Again only a few names are known: John Spiers, John Brooks, June Howard, June Harris, ? Hawkins, Margaretta Davies, Anne Saunders, Harold Lloyd and Michael Colbett.

Here Mr Griffiths is seen around 1922 sitting in the Walton bus that ran from the station to the town centre. On one occasion he was fined five shillings because one of his lights had gone out!

Form 9 of Ambleside Boys School on a visit to the Houses of Parliament in 1956. In the centre is the MP for Walton. Note the clothes the boys are wearing – these were the days of smart overcoats and gloves.

Children from Ashley Road School in the summer of 1952 are enjoying a visit to Hampton Court Palace.

Walton and Weybridge Council Offices, shortly after Princess Margaret opened them on 19 October 1966. The land had originally been purchased in 1938 to erect a public hall and fire station, but war intervened. In 1954 four acres were allocated for the building of civic offices, but the plans were not approved until 1962. Amongst those at the opening were visitors from Rueil-Malmaison (near Paris), the first to come to Walton under the new twinning scheme.

A rare glimpse into a Council meeting, showing the mayor, councillor Halcro Tait at work, and the interior of the civic office in 1977.

six

Walton's Film
Industry

Above: Film making began in Walton in 1899 under the trade name 'Hepwix' by Cecil Hepworth and his cousin Monty Wicks. They started in a villa, extreme left, rented for £36 per year, and became leading figures making silent pictures at Hurst Grove, now a 1960s shopping centre. Only the Playhouse, built as Hepworth's power house, remains. Hepworth drew the first covered studios at Walton around 1906.

Left: Cecil Hepworth is shown here in 1908 before he grew a moustache whilst an army officer. Amongst his many achievements was a continuous printing and developing machine, and an electrical device called the vivaphone, which synchronised the film projector with a gramophone record. Of around 2,000 films produced between 1899 and 1924, fewer than 200 survive. Hepworth also wrote *The ABC of Cinematography* in 1897, his first book on the subject and his autobiography *Came The Dawn,* in 1951. He died in 1953.

Above: Chrissie White and Henry Edwards are seen here pictured after their wedding at Chertsey Register Office in 1924. They avoided their fans by approaching in different directions, and walking the last 100 yards to the office. Chrissie is not wearing white, as she was divorced from Hepworth's studio manager, Claude Whitten. She began working for Hepworth when only twelve years old. Henry joined the company in 1915.

Right: This photograph taken by Elwin Neame shows the young Alma Taylor who worked for Hepworth from the age of twelve. There are two accounts of how she obtained her first job. One claims she went to the 'chemical factory' for a fancy dress revel, and impressed Hepworth with her personality. Another claims she caused a stir by joining in a football game with studio staff.

Following page: Alma Taylor seen here with her horse Chubby around 1920, lived in Esher Avenue in Walton. In his autobiography, Hepworth says that Alma was a natural actress who could cry real tears.

Above left: This postcard shows Chrissie White and Alma Taylor in *Tilly the Tomboy*, a series of nineteen comedies about two naughty schoolgirls made between 1910 and 1915. It was by playing the part of Sally that Chrissie made her name.

Above right: This scene is taken from the film *Comin' Thro' The Rye*, a 1923 Hepworth film. It was filmed in Ashley Park. Hepworth arranged for a field of rye to be sown to use at various stages of growth to symbolise the love affair, ranging from spring (falling in love) to winter (the betrayal caused by a jealous girl breaking up the heroine's engagement with a fake wedding announcement).

Right: Eileen Dennes first appeared for Hepworth with Gerald Ames, Mary Dibley and Alma Taylor in Sheba in 1919. This *Comin' Thro' The Rye* 1923 postcard is a scene from one of only three Hepworth publicised in this way. The film cost £10,000, failed to cover its cost and Hepworth went into bankruptcy. The negatives of Hepworth's films were sold and are now lost.

Left: Eric Desmond (real name Reginald Sheffield) first appeared on the stage as Michael Darling in *Peter Pan* at the Duke of York Theatre in London on 24 December 1912. His first film for Hepworth was David Copperfield in August 1913 and he went on to make another twenty-one films at Walton before going to America. His son, Johnny Sheffield, played Boy in the 1940s *Tarzan* series.

Right: Another couple that worked for Hepworth were Mary Dibley and Gerald Ames. Gerald began his film career with the London Film Company, Twickenham, in 1914, and joined Hepworth in 1918 making sixteen films in six years. Gerald was also a sportsman who represented England at fencing in the 1912 Olympic Games in Stockholm, reaching the semi-finals.

Right: Mary Dibley, seen here in 1916, like Gerald Ames first worked at the London Film Company. She made at least twenty films for Hepworth and her career spanned from 1912 to 1928. She and Gerald were divorced in 1918.

Left: Ivy Close, who was born in the same road in Stockton-on-Tees as Will Hay and, by winning the *Daily Mirror* competition in 1908, became the first English Beauty Queen. She married her photographer Elwin Neame, who photographed many of the actresses at Walton Film Studios.

The couple moved into a house in Bowes
Road and Ivy is pictured here with her sons.
Ronald, born in 1911 became a film producer,
and grandson Christopher is a film director.

After making a film called *Dream Painting*,
released in May 1912, which was developed
and printed by Hepworth, fifty copies were
sold. He offered them his studio facilities and
marketed the Ivy Close Films, as well as
employing her in his own productions. This
publicity photograph of Ivy Close was issued as
a Hepworth Stock Company postcard while
she was working for him.

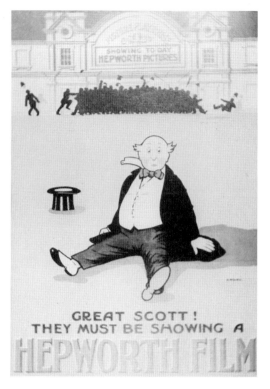

Above left: This is a typical poster of the Hepworth Film era.

Above right: Jack Hulcup, a singer in Edwardian musicals, was engaged by Hepworth for his Vivaphone pictures together with his wife, Claire Pridelle, and Edward Hay Plumb when Cecil heard them singing together at Walton Regatta. By 1912 Hepworth was making two vivaphone singing pictures a week although no catalogues can be found to verify this. Jack appeared in thirteen other Hepworth films between 1910 and 1915.

Right: Claire Pridelle made eighteen films at Walton between 1910 and 1914, which were probably made while she also sang for the Vivaphone films. This postcard is inscribed to William Felton who played villains for Hepworth Films.

Violet Hopson was born in San Francisco to British parents, but came to England as a baby. She began filming with Cecil Hepworth in 1912 and continued with him until 1919, appearing in over forty films. She married twice, including to Alec Worcester, another Hepworth star.

Stewart Rome (real name Septimus Wernham Ryott) trained as a civil engineer, but became a professional actor when he joined Hepworth in 1913. After the First World War he went to work for Broadwest Company under the name of Stewart Rome, which Hepworth had invented for him. Hepworth tried to prevent him from using it, but lost the case with the Court of Appeal ruling that this was a 'restraint of trade'.

This 1909 photograph shows the former post office in Church Street with a false front erected and bearing the inscription London & NE Bank for the making of the film *An Attempt to Smash a Bank*. The plot involved a rich man who, spurned by the banker's daughter, withdrew all his money. Often traffic was held up whilst filming in adverse weather conditions until Hepworth built his first indoor studio.

Crowd scenes were filmed on a Saturday morning when children were off school and they would be paid a shilling a day for appearing in a crowd. Scenes from Dickens *Barnaby Rudge* were shot in a little alleyway next to the Manor Public House. When these Dickens-like cottages were filmed, the occupants were paid, always welcome, particularly in winter.

Gladys Sylvani began working with Hepworth in *The Heart of a Fisher Girl* in December 1910. A Hepworth letter, dated 3 July 1911, offers her a year's contract at £5 per week, apparently the oldest British film contract. According to Bioscope, 2 May 1912, she was the most popular English picture actress that year. She made forty-four films at Walton before ending her career in late 1912.

Flora Morris appeared in over fifty films with Hepworth between 1910 and 1914, her peak year being 1913 when she appeared in twenty-two, none of which made her a name. However Hepworth did publicise her on his Hepworth Stock Company postcards in four different poses, the same number allocated to Alma Taylor and Chrissie White.

Ronald Colman, seen here in a *Tale of Two Cities*, had been on the stage and after being invalided out of the First World War worked with Hepworth in a handful of films, including probably with Alma Taylor in *Anne the Adventuress*, February 1921, where Hepworth's split-screen technique shows her as twin sisters. He went to America where he became a romantic actor.

Forbes Robertson's most famous role, as Hamlet, was also his first film. It was made by the Hepworth Company under the direction of Edward Hay Plumb who also acted and directed in a career lasting until 1939.

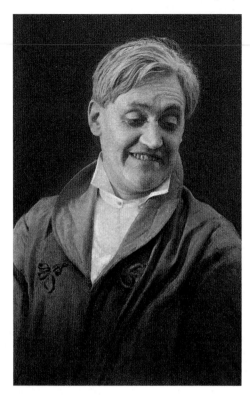

Left: Henry Anley made six Hepworth silent films between 1914 and 1916. In this postcard we see him in the role of Dick Phenyl in Sweet Lavender, a part he was especially engaged to play.

Right: After Hepworth studios were sold to Archibald Nettleford, the transition from silent to sound films was made. In the 1950s, Sapphire films, which had a stake in the studios, produced 143 half-hour episodes of *Robin Hood* starring Richard Greene, seen here around 1955. This popular series is reported to have been seen in 1957 by 70 million viewers each week in Britain, America and Canada.

seven

Wartime

The entrance to Mount Felix around 1916 with the distinctive Clock Tower in the background. This was the second of the New Zealand hospitals to be established in the UK when the New Zealand War Contingent Association took it over in June 1915 and opened it at the end of July. By September, responsibility was passed to the Army Medical Services who gave it the title New Zealand No. 2 General Hospital.

To expand accommodation, five huts – each for forty soldiers, were erected in January 1916 on the land between Oatlands Drive and the River Thames on the opposite side of the road. A footbridge was built to link the two sites, seen here in 1917 from the approach to Walton Bridge. Note on the left of the picture one of the iron city wine and coal posts marking the boundary of the Metropolitan Police District.

Right: This photograph taken in the 1970s shows the same post incorporating the Corporation of London crest, at its original boundary setting. In order to cover the costs of re-building after the Great Fire of London (1666) the Corporation of London was allowed until 1861 to levy a charge on coal entering London. The Inscription 24 & 25 VIC CAP 42 indicates the boundary was set up in accordance with the Act of Parliament in the 24th and 25th years of Queen Victoria's reign, charter 42 of the Statute Book.

Below: This photograph of Ward Four in 1916 shows soldiers recuperating in an airy atmosphere. Although run by the military authorities, the hospital was in part staffed by Voluntary Aid Detachments (VADs), until nurses could be trained and sent from New Zealand. Between 1915-19 a total of 23,000 patients were treated at Mount Felix.

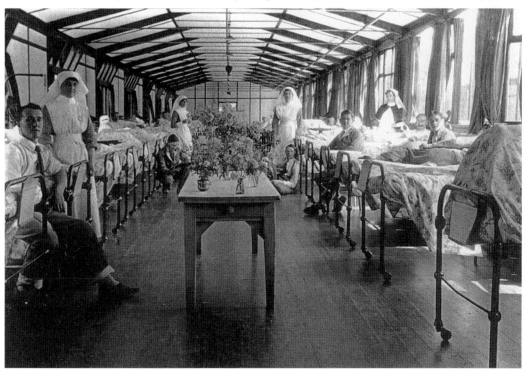

The Mess Room, around 1917, was set up in one of the huts to provide a cosy dining area for those who were well enough to enjoy a meal away from the wards.

New Zealand soldiers outside the Bear around 1919. Under strict rules they were not allowed to consume alcohol at Mount Felix and we can assume that a visit to the Bear was a rare treat, or the soldiers may only be posing outside for a photograph.

Above and below: These two photographs taken between 1916 and 1918 show New Zealand soldiers, nicknamed 'the boys in blue' because of their distinctive pale blue uniforms, enjoying sports day in the grounds of Mount Felix. The picture above shows the nurses enjoying a game of Tug of War, whilst below the soldiers look on as the nurses race each other in an egg and spoon race.

This postcard, by Berks of Bridge Street, shows the soldiers standing on the bridge linking the two hospital sites. Below is one of the shelters that could be rotated to face the sun or away from the wind and rain. They were known as the Lord Plunket shelters, and each could accommodate one person.

Over 3,000 people watched as the war memorial to Walton's 130 war dead was unveiled on Sunday 10 July 1921. It was a hot summer's day with temperatures reaching 128 degrees fahrenheit – hence the parasols and headgear. The Earl Beatty unveiled the memorial, consisting of inscribed panels mounted on Portland Stone. Revd B. Stanley, a Wesleyan minister, and Revd Kemp Bussell, of St Mary's, conducted the service. A bugler from the 6th Batt. East Surrey Regiment sounded the last post.

In commemoration of the signing of the Peace Treaty in Versailles after the great war, the directors and staff of Claudius Ash and Sons Co. Ltd are seen on a staff outing to Brighton, 6 September 1919. Edward Power, a local Councillor, was managing director.

Staff from Mount Felix taking a break from nursing duties are pictured here in 1917 enjoying a day of boating on the River Thames.

A member of the Walton-on-Thames 79 Battery LAA, RA is seen here at Kempton Water Works in late 1939 holding a 303 Lee Enfield rifle.

At around 7.30 p.m. on 9 November 1940 eight bombs fell between Rydens Avenue and the River Mole. A direct hit on a pair of semi-detached houses resulted in a lucky escape for one resident and his wife. They had been sitting in the back of the house when the bedroom floor collapsed and formed a triangular space over them, leaving them dirty but unharmed. This picture was taken in June 1941 after some repair work had been carried out.

Above: After Anthony Eden, the Secretary of State for War, appealed for 'volunteers to do their bit for their country,' the Local Defence Volunteers (LDV) or Home Guard was born. An offshoot of this became the Upper Thames Patrol (UTP) who covered the 125-mile length of the river in privately owned motor launches. This photograph taken around 1942 shows the Upper Thames Patrol, the first inland water patrol to be officially received by the newly formed LDV.

Right: Pictured here is the Upper Thames Patrol badge, *c.* 1942. Volunteers were not paid, but a uniform was supplied.

Victory in Europe (VE Day) was celebrated all over Walton in street parties which usually ended in games and dancing. This photograph, taken in May 1945, shows the residents of Rydens Road enjoying themselves.

The residents of Florence Road contributed whatever they could spare from their rations to ensure they celebrated VE Day with a good party.

eight

At work...
at play

This photograph taken around 1900 shows the milk being delivered to the Swan. At this time there were two deliveries of milk a day, one morning, one afternoon, and sometimes a third delivery, called the pudding round, to the bigger houses. Older residents talk of a side door to Triggs dairy, fitted with a slot machine, where a penny delivered a pint of milk into the customer's jug. To ensure the milk was of a legal standard, a plunger had to be pressed to 'stir' the milk as cream rises to the top.

This picture shows a hive of activity at the polishing shop of Claudius Ash Dental Factory, *c.* 1914. At this time, the factory employed around 100 people. On the workbench can be seen the probes, known as Ash's Root elevators. The factory became the leading manufacturer of dental surgical instruments with a worldwide market.

This photograph taken around 1967 shows rows of dental chairs inside the Amalgamated Dental Factory ready for delivery. The factory was a major employer in the area, with around 1,000 workers. The firm were amongst the first to adopt chromium plating, and developed fibre optics in dentistry. On reorganisation the name was changed in 1968 to AD Engineering Co. and closed on 27 November 1981.

The swimming pool, built in 1967 off King's Close, was designed by Ove Arup and was credited in Pervsner and Nairn Survey of Surrey as being Walton's best modern building.

St Mary's Youth Fellowship are seen here in a scene from *Meet The Family* May 1939. From left to right: Rosaline Ayley, Pat Griffin, Grace Winter, Enid Mole (secretary), Roy Taylor, Jimmy Walker, Victor Hall, Joan Griffin, John Ridgewell, and Fred Johnson (treasurer). The producer Jimmy Goode is not pictured.

Tents erected on the green by the Civic Hall in New Zealand Avenue during the Church in Action Week celebrations in 1974 that were organised by local churches. The lighting inside the tents gives this unusual effect.

Children are seen here enjoying the music during the Church in Action Week celebrations in 1974.

June Harris (middle of the three ladies) is busy at work in the Clock Tower in 1959. Shirley Barton, the receptionist, occupies the first seat. These were the offices of Kenneth G. Haynes who ran a wholesale business importing pet foods as well as owning the Pet Shop in New Zealand Avenue.

Above: Here we see the mayor of Elmbridge and the vicar of St Mary's at work during an Anzac day service in 1977. From left to right are: the High Commissioner of New Zealand, Mrs Seyler, Mayor Cllr Alan E. Charlton and his wife, Revd Tony Carter and Keith Seyler who organised the service.

Left: Sister Geraldine Harvey working at Walton Hospital instructing agency nurses. Sister Harvey worked at the hospital from 1958 to 1979.

Ronald Tickner organised charabanc trips from Walton to Brighton and Southsea. A typical outing seen here around 1920, shows that the charabancs were usually underpowered and overloaded, which meant that when a steep climb was encountered, such as Berry Hill on the way to Brighton, the men had to get out and push. Another notorious blackspot was Newlands corner, near Guildford. This time women and children had to get out and walk, whilst the men pushed.

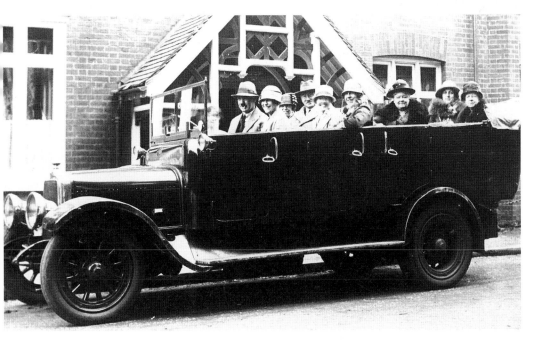

In this 1919 photograph we see a party waiting outside the Swan Hotel before leaving for the Epsom Derby.

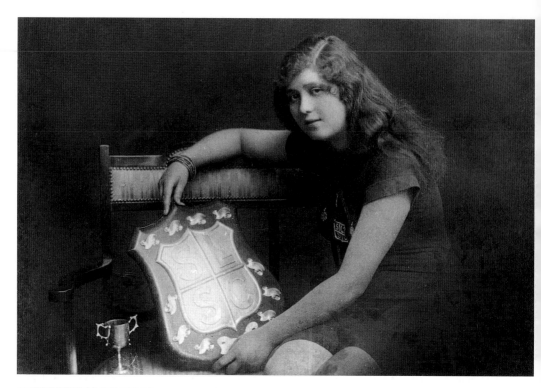

Above: Pansy Irene Seaby holds the Surrey Ladies Swimming Club Shield at Walton-on-Thames in 1913/14. The daughter of John Seaby who ran the 'fly' business, she was often used as an extra in Hepworth films.

Left: This drawing of the first purpose-built cinema dates from 1915, the same year as the readers of *Picturegoer* magazine named Alma Taylor as best actress of the year. Another Walton actress Chrissie White came fifth.

The Capitol opened in 1927, on the site of the present Screen Cinema. This photograph taken in 1931 shows the roof display to publicise Hell's Angels starring Jean Harlow.

This photograph shows children waiting for the steamboat to take them on a Sunday school outing to Windsor, *c.* 1920. In the picture, Jack Rosewell and Arthur Grant are seated.

Architect George Carvill bought the building that Hepworth used to store his electricity generators and turned it into a small theatre, the Playhouse. The Foundation stone was laid on 7 September 1925, tapped into place by Dame Ellen Terry with a silver trowel presented to her by Alma (Taylor) Cooper, star of *Comin' through the Rye*. In the photograph is George Carvill with trowel in hand, Dame Ellen Terry, the famous Shakespearian actress, Alma, Mr and Mrs Morris, Mrs and Mrs Trigg, and Miss Tidd(?).

The Playhouse opened in December 1925 with a performance of the Mikado presented by the Walton Players (later to become the Amateur Operatic Society) with Hepworth as musical director. This photograph shows a scene from another play performed at the Playhouse, *c.* 1925-1930.

Whilst working at the record department at Birkheads in Church Street, Deniz Corday realised that the youth of Walton wanted to be part of the rock and roll scene that was sweeping the country. He hired the Playhouse for a night on 3 June 1958 and with a borrowed record player and speakers entertained 400 youngsters. From those humble beginnings Walton 'Hop' was born. This photograph, taken in 1960, shows youngsters enjoying one of these sessions, which took place three times a week, in the days when no alcohol was served.

nine

Religion

This postcard of St Mary's Church and Church Walk was taken by Edmund Jordon, *c.* 1910. Off picture is the new church hall, opened in December 1903 by the Duchess of Albany, King Edward's VII's sister-in-law, who lived at Claremont in Esher.

This photograph shows the interior of St Mary's at the turn of the century. The pulpit, still in use, was presented to the Church in 1902 by Fanny Gill of Apps Court in memory of husband Robert, and daughter Madeline Lucy. Also in view is one of the two brass chandeliers that then hung in the Church.

Right: This more modern photograph of the interior taken around 1970 shows the five Norman pillars with fluted capitals. On the column next to the pulpit there is a rhyme, attributed to Queen Elizabeth I. It reads:

Christ was the Worde and spake it
He took the Bread and brake it
And what the Worde doth make it
That I believe, and take it.

Above left: Although out of scale to the rest of the church, the Shannon Memorial is the finest memorial in St Mary's. Lady Shannon of Ashley Park left £1,000 in her will for a memorial to her husband, Field Marshall Richard Boyle, Viscount Shannon. Walton Vestry granted permission for the memorial to be built, but it caused a rift in the parish that took many years to heal.

Above right: This photograph also taken in the 1970s is a close up of the memorial to Viscount Shannon who spent fifty years in the army. It was created by Louis Roubilliac, is of national and European importance, and shows the Viscount against a background of a tent, leaning on a mortar. The figure at his feet is probably modelled on Roubilliac's third wife.

Left: The organ in the west gallery was originally built in 1673 by the King's organ maker, Bernard Smith, for the King's private chapel in Windsor Castle and came to St Mary's in 1711. A new organ was installed in 1936, but the casing and some of Smith's prospect pipes were retained. When Sir Arthur Sullivan, of Gilbert and Sullivan fame, lived at the Riverhouse during the 1880-90s, he occasionally played on the organ.

Right: The oldest memorial in St Mary's, dated 1587, is a five-part Selwyn brass, set into the north wall. This commemorates John Selwyn, Queen Elizabeth's gamekeeper at Oatlands Park. This photograph shows the smallest and most interesting of the brasses. According to legend this tells of an incident in Oatlands Park when a stag ran towards the Queen. John reacted quickly and jumped from his horse onto the back of the stag and killed it.

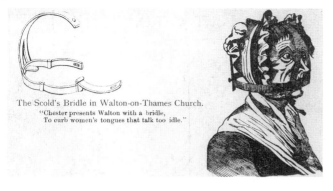

The Scold's Bridle in Walton-on-Thames Church.
"Chester presents Walton with a bridle,
To curb women's tongues that talk too idle."

THE "SCOLD'S" OR
THE GOSSIP'S BRIDLE
IN
WALTON CHURCH

"Chester presents Walton with a Bridle

To curb women's tongues that talk too idle."

WALTON CHURCH   COPYRIGHT

Above and right: These postcards show the scold's bridle, a curious contraption that dates to 1633. Unfortunately it was stolen from the church in 1965 and has been replaced by a replica. According to legend the 'Chester' referred to in the rhyme was a man who is supposed to have lost an estate through women gossiping about his affairs.

Left: St John's, the daughter church of St Mary's, seen here in the 1970s, was built on a plot of land gifted in 1939 by Mrs Eva Drabble. Mrs Drabble also gave a window in memory of her parents and is commemorated by the alter rail in the All Saints Chapel. Fund-raising for the new church was delayed during wartime and building eventually started in 1953.

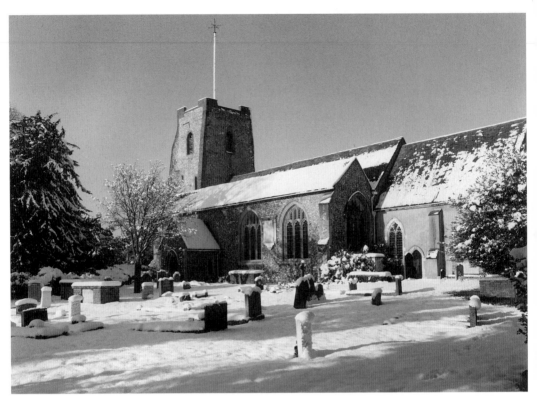

This 1970s photograph shows St Mary's Church with a covering of snow.

The most significant graves in Walton are those of the twenty-one New Zealand Army personnel, photographed around the 1970s, who were nursed and died at Mount Felix during the First World War. New Zealand has never forgotten the kindness of Walton people to the soldiers wounded at Gallipoli and a strong connection still exists.

An Anzac Day service is held annually at St Mary's to commemorate those New Zealand soldiers who died in Walton during the First World War. This photograph, taken after the 1977 service, shows from left to right: Mr Keith Seyler, Mrs Aston, Cllr Hugh Aston, Mayor of Elmbridge, Revd John Moore, Revd Canon Timothy Sedgley and Mr Chilton, Acting High Commissioner for New Zealand.

This unusual stone pyramid grave in Walton Cemetery commemorates Mary Fredrick who died on 18 November 1794 aged thirty-five, and is buried in St Olave Jewry Church in London. She was the wife of Sir John Fredrick Bart of Burwood Park who died on 16 January 1825 aged seventy-six, whose remains are deposited in the vault. The inscription on it says that Sir John represented the county in five parliaments.

Left: This gravestone was erected by public subscription in memory of PC 356 Fred Atkins, a Walton resident who was attached to Kingston Police Station. On 22 September 1881 he was shot three times by an unknown assailant, whilst inspecting a large house on Kingston Hill and died the following day, aged twenty-three. The funeral was one of the most impressive Walton has seen, attended by nearly 2,000 police officers and the V division band playing the 'Dead March' from Saul.

Below: The Methodists established in 1845 a chapel in Back Street, which became known as Chapel Street, and is now Manor Road. In 1887 a new chapel was built in Terrace Road, and this photograph of the interior of that chapel was taken after the removal of the pipe organ from the east end in 1970.

The local Presbyterians, who had been hiring the Playhouse for a weekly service since 1928, acquired land in Hersham Road when 'The Chestnuts' was sold for redevelopment. P.G. Overall designed a church to seat 350, and a hall to seat 250. The Revd Hugh Macluskie was appointed acting minister in March 1931, and Lord Beaverbrook laid the foundation stone in November 1931. W.H. Gaze and Sons, of Bridge Street began building work on 20 February 1932 and their Works Band played at the opening ceremony. The intended church was never constructed, and this photograph shows the hall, which remains in use by the United Reformed Church, c. 1935.

This photograph shows the interior of the United Reformed Church with the Revd William McCrorie conducting a wedding service, c. 1970.

The Roman Catholic Church in Esher Avenue, shown here around 1920, is dedicated to St Erconwald founder of Chertsey Abbey. Designed by local architect, G.B. Cavill, the first public mass since the Reformation was celebrated on Sunday 30 May 1906.

This photograph of a wedding service shows the interior of St Erconwald's in the new larger church, consecrated in 1937. The old church remains as a church hall.

ten

People and Events

Arthur and William Hirons worked for Miskin's from 1898. This photograph of the younger Mr Hirons (presumably William), taken soon after, shows him with one of Miskin's horse and carts. In an interview, conducted in the 1950s when William was eighty-five, he recalled that a few months after joining the company part of the first barge-load of timber to be unloaded at Walton Wharf fell on him. This crushed his leg, breaking his ankle and resulted in his only sick leave during his whole working career.

This photograph taken in 1894 shows Alfred, Joseph Sassoon's younger brother with his children. Far left is Siegfried Sassoon, the First World War poet. Alfred and his sister Rachel married outside the Jewish faith and were disowned by their mother. Legend says Rachel's picture at Ashley Park was turned to face the wall as a result of her marriage.

This slightly damaged photograph taken in 1897 shows the seven children of Joseph and Louise Sassoon outside Ashley Park House. They are from left to right: Mozelle, Missy, Freddie, Arthur, Totts and twins Teddy and David.

Local school children celebrated the coronation of King George V on 22 June 1911 at Ashley Park.

The Walton Drum and Fife band are seen here celebrating the Relief of Mafeking 24 May 1900. John Seaby is on the far left dressed in a coachman's costume.

Esther Mary and Louis Phillipe Millican, seen here around 1900, came to Walton in 1875 and opened a bakery in Hersham Road. All six of his children helped in the shop.

Above: The Millican family,
c. 1919. From left to right,
standing: Percy Starling, Revd
Fisher, (Lucy Millican) Starling,
Will Sharp, Bert Millican, Arthur
Sharp. Next row, seated: Hilda
Mary Ann Millican (married
A.L. Howard) Nell Sharp (née
Milllican) Esther Mary Ann
Millican (née Cox) Alfred
Millican, Annie Millican (who
married a Fisher) and seated in
front, Winn Sharp and Margery
Starling.

Right: The photograph taken on
8 August 1901 to celebrate
Edward VII's coronation shows
the decorations at the junction of
Church Street and Bridge Street.
On the right can be seen John
Bristow's furniture shop, which
had been in operation since the
1880s. In front is the
headquarters of Annett and Son,
builders, and Annett's china shop.

Above: This photograph is of Ashley Road School's Boys Brigade, *c.* 1915.

Left: In 1516 Henry VIII granted a licence to Walton-on-Thames to hold fairs, an important trading concession, on Tuesday and Wednesday in Easter week, and on the 3 and 4 October each year. The Easter Fair survived until 1879 when it was abolished by a Council order following a request from the Walton Vestry that it had become 'a great nuisance'. The October fair seems to have ceased long before this date.

Above: An attempt was made to revive the Goose Fair in the 1970s, and this picture shows 'Henry VIII' enjoying a drink and a chat with his subjects.

Right: Here we see the Morris dancers entertaining the crowd at the same fair. Unfortunately the revival of this ancient fair did not last for long.

Left: Bill Wright, Walton's talented cartoonist seen here at the Goose Fair in 1976; note his drawing of Henry VIII on the table. The Walton Review of August 1956 reported that the George Public House in Bridge Street had a gallery of drawings by Walton's sports cartoonist, Bill Wright.

Below: Gladys Ward came to Walton in 1898 and until her mother died, she always wore black in memory of her two brothers, killed in the First World War. She was a keen rower as this picture in the 1950s shows and often would row from Walton to Windsor and back. In 1969 she sold her boat to a Staines man.

Right: This photograph, taken in the 1970s, shows Gladys Ward (who died in 1976) tending an Easter garden in All Saints Chapel of St Mary's. Above her head can be seen the memorial to Alison Jardine (mother of the cricket captain D.R. Jardine) who died in 1936.

Below: After several weeks of heavy rain – more than three inches fell in twenty-four hours over the weekend of 14/15 September 1968. The following day the river Mole burst its banks at Esher Road, Hersham and water flowed three-feet deep though the railway bridge, into Walton Park and reached the Cottimore area by mid-afternoon. Franks Wheals of the Clerks Department can be seen here rowing down Florence Road.

Left: As part of the celebrations to mark the coronation of King Edward VII in 1901, a fair was held at Ashley Park. Seen here are some of the local children enjoying the event. The lady in the hat in front of the little girl on the right is Mrs Drabble, who with her husband Dr Drabble contributed so much to the amenities of Walton.

Below: Members of St Mary's Church enjoying a Harvest Supper at the church hall, *c.* 1974.

Right: This photograph taken by Harold Whittingham of Walton-on-Thames shows the winners of the Skiff Marathon, Putney to Mortlake 1930 and 1931. In the picture are Joe Barnley, Bum Croucher and Jack Rosewell far right.

Left: Frank Rosewell of Rosewell's boatyard taken around 1932.

Left: Mr John Seaby who ran his horse-drawn fly business from Church Street, *c.* 1920. When his two sons were killed in the First World War, his wife led a group to attack the premises of Mr Hillbrand, a German jeweller and clockmaker. The situation was only resolved when Mr Keswick, MP for Walton, read the Riot Act from a horse bus at the corner of Church Street.

Below: Waiting for the next train to arrive, outside Walton Taxi rank around the 1930s is Mr Seaby, the large man with a top hat. Next to him is Mr Smart, Mr Griffiths, driver of the Walton bus, Mr Paulter, Mr Barker, and Mr Harry Griffiths.

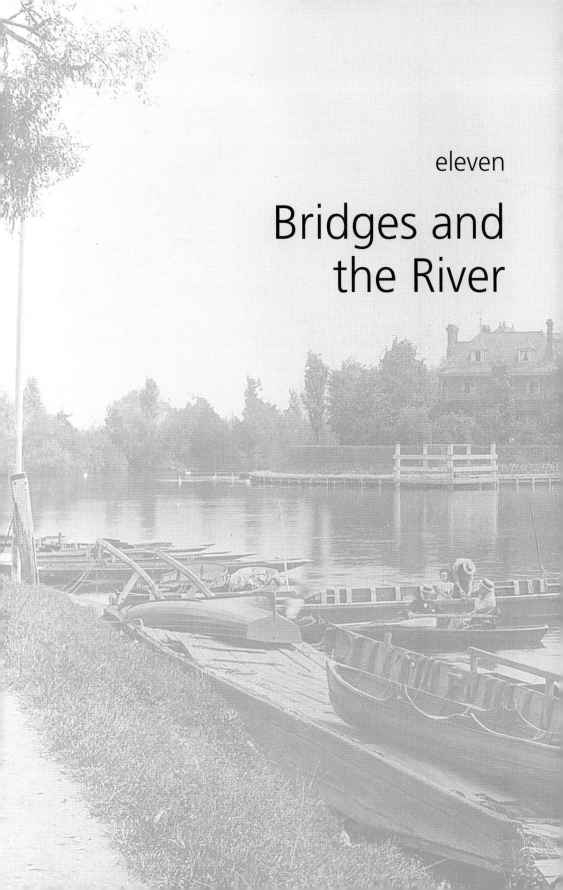

eleven

Bridges and the River

Cowey Sale, derived from the seventeenth-century Cow Way and a small stream known as Seale or Sale, is a twenty-acre stretch of riverside land by Walton Bridge. It was used for grazing and was approached by a wooden bridge as this eighteenth-century engraving shows. Cowey Stakes, named in the sixteenth century after wooden stakes found in the riverbed, was an old ford across the Thames about 200 yards upstream from Walton Bridge. In the 1580s William Camden ascertained that Julius Caesar crossed the Thames during his second invasion in 54 BC and, according to Caesar, when opposed by the Britons drove stakes into the riverbed as a defence.

Until the eighteenth century the river could only be crossed by ferry, although when the water was low, there was a ford a little upstream of the present bridge. In 1744 Samuel Dicker, a wealthy Jamaican plantation owner and MP acquired land on what later became Mount Felix. After meeting local opposition, he secured a private act of parliament authorising him to build a bridge and charge tolls. The first bridge, possibly designed by William Etheridge, was opened in 1750 and visitors came from all around to look at the wooden arched structure. Engravings, such as this, dated 1752, were widely published and Canaletto painted two pictures of the bridge.

In 1799 Dicker's nephew, Michael Dicker Sanders, replaced the bridge. This was designed by John Paine of Addlestone and constructed with brick and stone. It was praised for its appearance, and even J.M.W. Turner painted a picture of it. On 11 August 1859 the central section collapsed into the Thames as seen in this sketch by Mr P. Duggan. It was replaced in 1863 by a flat iron structure with four spans on solid piers and remained a private toll bridge until 1870 when it was declared a free county bridge. The iron bridge was damaged during the war and declared unsafe for traffic in 1953.

This close up from the 1970s shows the arches of Walton's fourth bridge. The third and fourth bridges stood side-by-side from the 1950s until the iron bridge was finally pulled down in 1985.

Above: The first Walton Regatta was held in 1862 and this photograph from around 1908 gives the general view of the course. The grounds of Mount Felix were opened for the day and chairs were provided for spectators to enjoy the event, and sometimes a band. Window boxes were decorated and banners and streamers spanned High Street and Bridge Street.

Left: This aerial photograph of the River Thames taken in 1931 shows the distinctive Italian shape of Mount Felix centre right of picture. Towards the top of the picture, far right, can be seen Riverhouse, which at the end of the nineteenth century was the occasional home of Sir Arthur Sullivan. At the time of this photograph the MP for Walton, Archibald Boyd-Carpenter, lived here.

This photograph from the 1920s of Rosewell's boatyard shows the many punts and skiffs for hire. To the right can been seen the iron bridge, sometimes known as horse bridge used by the barge-horses to cross the backwater.

The towpath has always been a popular walk for young and old. This photograph taken in 1970 shows two little girls enjoying a walk with a Jack Russell terrier.

This photograph, taken in the 1930s, shows anglers enjoying a quiet day fishing. The far bank shows Mount Felix gardens with the house off picture to the right.

This postcard taken around 1936 shows the Rosewell family. A party of young ladies is paying Frank Rosewell for hire of a punt, whilst his son, Jim Rosewell is seen sitting on a boat trolley with his back to the river wearing a white shirt.

Right: The river has always been a huge attraction, even at night as this 1970s photograph shows with the moon providing enough light for these late night anglers and lone rower.

Below: D'Oyly Carte island, photographed in the 1930s, originally a sandbank in the Thames, was chosen by the Rupert D'Oyly Carte (Savoy Opera fame) as the site for a summer annexe for the Savoy Hotel in London which he owned. Unable to secure a licence for the premises, he lived there himself and the island became a meeting and rehearsal place for his son, Richard's operatic associates.

This photograph shows just how popular the river can be, *c.* 1910. Across the river is Clark's boatyard, The Anglers, and the entrance to the Swan. Far right is Back Lane, which led down to the wharf where carts would come to be loaded.

This is Rosewell's boatyard in about 1910 by the backwater, established by John Roswell's eldest son Sedgwick around 1885. An advertisement of the period claims that the boathouse was patronised by the present Emperor and Empress of Russia. This relates to the time when the future Tsar and Tsarina stayed with Prince Louis at Elm Grove in 1894. Walton Marina now occupies the area. Walton Bridge can be seen in the distance spanning the Thames.

This photograph from Fricker Photos of Esher, shows the wharf at the beginning of the twentieth century. Barges, including those that carried coal for the Walton-on-Thames and Weybridge Gas Company, would have been loaded and unloaded here. Beyond the Swan and Anglers can be seen Rosewell's lower boathouse before a second storey was added between 1904 and 1908. William Hirons remembers seeing touring circuses, and elephants from the shows being led through Walton to the public draw-dock by the Swan. Unfortunately, the boatmen could not claim compensation for damage caused by the animals.

Members of the Thames Camping and Boating Association seen here enjoying a weekend at the camping ground opposite the Weir Hotel, c. 1909. The campers would order provisions from the local grocery shops taking with them what they needed for that day. The shop's delivery boys would work from 7 a.m. in the morning and would hire a boat to deliver the remainder of the groceries before breakfast. They would also run errands to fetch water from the boathouse and other necessities, in exchange for payment and free boating, always an attraction for the youngsters of Walton.

Walton Bathing Pavilion was erected on the towpath between the Anglers and Sunbury Lane in 1909 and extended three years later. This 1916 photograph shows the staff and soldiers at No. 2 New Zealand General Hospital enjoying the local facilities.

This postcard, postmarked 24 December 1907, shows the old Walton badge surrounded by various views of Walton and is typical of the type of card sent by visitors to friends and family.